HYDROGEN AND THE NOBLE GASES

A TRUE BOOK®

by

Salvatore Tocci

Children's Press®

A Division of Scholastic Inc.

New York Toronto London Auckland Sydney
Mexico City New Delhi Hong Kong
Danbury, Connecticut

Margarine is made when hydrogen gas is bubbled through vegetable oil.

Reading Consultant
Julia McKenzie Munemo, EdM
New York, New York

Content Consultant
John A. Benner
Austin, Texas

The photo on the cover shows balloons filled with helium. The photo on the title page shows a neon sign.

The author and the publisher are not responsible for injuries or accidents that occur during or from any experiments. Experiments should be conducted in the presence of or with the help of an adult. Any instructions of the experiments that require the use of sharp, hot, or other unsafe items should be conducted by or with the help of an adult.

Library of Congress Cataloging-in-Publication Data

Tocci, Salvatore.
Hydrogen and the noble gases / by Salvatore Tocci.
   p. cm. — (A true book)
   Includes bibliographical references and index.
   Contents: Why does it fly?—What is hydrogen?—What are the noble gases?—Why are they so different?—Fun facts about hydrogen and the noble gases.
   ISBN 0-516-22830-7 (lib. bdg.)   0-516-27849-5 (pbk.)
   1. Hydrogen—Juvenile literature. 2. Gases, Rare—Juvenile literature. [1. Hydrogen. 2. Gases, Rare.] I. Title. II. Series.
QD181.H1T63 2004
546'.21—dc22   2003016211

CHILDREN'S PRESS, and A TRUE BOOK™, and associated logos are trademarks and or registered trademarks of Scholastic Library Publishing. SCHOLASTIC and associated logos are trademarks and or registered trademarks of Scholastic Inc.

1 2 3 4 5 6 7 8 9 10 R 13 12 11 10 09 08 07 06 05 04

Contents

The *Hindenburg* was the largest aircraft that has ever flown. It was more than 800 feet (240 meters) long, or almost as long as the *Titanic*.

Why Does It Fly?

Have you ever seen a blimp moving slowly across the sky? A blimp is a large, football-shaped bag filled with gas. In 1937, a German blimp named the *Hindenburg* had just crossed the Atlantic Ocean and was heading for New Jersey. Just before landing, the tail of the *Hindenburg* burst into flames. Within seconds, the whole blimp was on fire. Fortunately, sixty-one of the ninety-seven people on board were saved.

Modern blimps have a length that is only slightly larger than the distance around the middle of the *Hindenburg*. Although they are much smaller, modern blimps do have something in common with the *Hindenburg*. All blimps are filled with a gas

A modern blimp is about 200 feet (60 m) long, or one-quarter the length of the *Hindenburg*.

that is lighter than air. This allows them to fly.

Fortunately, modern blimps cannot burst into flames like

the *Hindenburg* did. Blimps today are filled with helium gas. The *Hindenburg* was filled with hydrogen gas. Both hydrogen and helium gases are lighter than air and allow blimps to fly.

However, there is one important difference between hydrogen and helium gases. Hydrogen gas is extremely explosive. In contrast, helium gas will not even spark if a match is lit.

What Is Hydrogen?

Hydrogen is an **element**. An element is the building block of matter. **Matter** is the stuff or material that makes up everything in the universe. This book, the chair you are sitting on, and even your body are made of matter.

There are millions of different kinds of matter. However, there are just a few more than one hundred different elements. How can so many different kinds of matter be made up of so few elements? Think about the English language. Just twenty-six letters can be arranged to make up all the words in the language. Likewise, the approximately one hundred different elements can be combined in

Hydrogen is the most abundant element in the universe, but is only the tenth most abundant element on Earth.

different ways to make up all the different kinds of matter in the universe.

The word "hydrogen" comes from two Greek words: *hydro,* which means water, and *genes,* which means maker. Hydrogen, then, means "water maker." Hydrogen was given its name by French scientist Antoine Lavoisier in 1788. He noticed that water droplets were made when hydrogen was burned in air. In addition to a name, every element has a symbol. The symbol for hydrogen is H, the first letter in its name.

French scientist Antoine Lavoisier gave hydrogen its name.

Making Hydrogen

If hydrogen is used to make water, you should be able to remove hydrogen from water. Fill a small glass with water. Add 2 teaspoons of table salt and stir until all the salt dissolves. Cut two 6-inch (15-centimeter) pieces of bare copper wire. Wrap one end of each wire around the terminals of a 9-volt battery. Dip the free ends of the wire into the water. Make sure they do not touch. Look for the hydrogen gas bubbles that rise to the surface of the water.

Hydrogen is one of the two elements that make up water. The other element is oxygen.

Although hydrogen is found everywhere on Earth, it is rarely found by itself. Hydrogen combines easily with other elements to form **compounds**. A compound is a substance that is a combination of two or more different elements. Compounds that contain hydrogen include water, coal, and natural gas. Pure hydrogen can be extracted from these compounds. Getting the hydrogen out of a compound is not a simple job. For example, natural gas must be heated as high as 1800 degrees Fahrenheit

(1000 degrees Celsius) to extract the hydrogen.

The hydrogen extracted from these compounds has many uses. The most common use for hydrogen is as an ingredient in fertilizers for crops and gardens. Hydrogen is also used to make margarine, which is done by bubbling hydrogen gas through vegetable oil. Hydrogen turns the oil, which is a liquid, into margarine,

About fifty tanker trucks are needed to transport the hydrogen fuel from Louisiana, where it is made, to Florida to launch each space shuttle.

which is a solid. Hydrogen is also used as a fuel to launch the space shuttle.

Scientists are looking for ways to use hydrogen to supply power for cars and other vehicles. The power would be supplied by a **hydrogen fuel cell**. These fuel cells would have several advantages when compared with engines that burn gasoline and diesel fuel. Burning gasoline and diesel fuel causes air pollution. A hydrogen fuel cell gives off water, but not pollution. A hydrogen fuel cell

This sport utility vehicle is powered by a hydrogen fuel cell.

would also be much more efficient at producing energy than the engines used today.

Hydrogen fuel cells have been tested in cars, buses, trucks, motor scooters, and boats. Even airplanes and submarines are being designed and built to run on power that comes from hydrogen fuel cells. The hydrogen is kept in sturdy and safe containers so that it will not explode and cause a disaster like the one that destroyed the *Hindenburg*.

What Are the Noble Gases?

Like hydrogen, helium is an element. Helium belongs to a group of elements that share certain things in common. For example, these elements have no color, odor, or taste. These elements belong to a group called the **noble gases,** which includes helium,

Helium was first discovered in 1868 when a scientist was studying sunlight as the moon passed between the sun and Earth.

neon, argon, krypton, xenon, and radon.

The word "helium" comes from the Greek word *helios*, which means sun. Scientists

Rising and Falling

Besides helium, hot air is also used to lift balloons into the sky. To see how heating the air causes a balloon to rise, get a shiny foil balloon filled with helium. Let out some of the helium so that the balloon hangs in the air and does not rise or fall when you let it go. Place the balloon so that it floats just above a bare lightbulb. Turn on the bulb so that the heat from the light warms the helium inside the balloon. The balloon should inflate a little and slowly rise into the air. As the helium inside the balloon cools, the balloon should start to fall.

first discovered helium on the sun and later found it on Earth. Helium, whose symbol is He, is the second most abundant element in the universe. On Earth, helium is found in tiny amounts in the air. Besides being used in blimps, helium is also mixed with oxygen gas and used by divers who need to breathe while under water.

Neon is most often used in advertising signs because

it gives off a bright, reddish light when electricity is passed through it. The symbol for neon is Ne. Whenever you see a glowing red sign, it is most likely filled with neon. You probably have seen neon in a super-market. The red light that is used to scan the bar codes on products contains neon gas. Neon is also used to make flat-screen televisions called plasma TVs.

Neon is used to make television screens that take up much less space than television screens made from traditional components.

The noble gases argon (Ar), krypton (Kr), and xenon (Xe) are mainly used in lights. When you look closely at a lightbulb, you will see a thin wire inside the glass. Except for the wire, the glass bulb looks empty. Actually, the bulb is filled with argon gas that keeps the thin wire from burning up when it gets hot. Krypton is used in the flashing lights that outline airport runways. Xenon is used in a car's headlights to produce a

The space shuttle has no landing lights. It depends on the xenon lights that light up the runway.

powerful white light that makes it easier for drivers to read road signs at night. Xenon lights are also used to light the runway whenever the space shuttle lands at night.

Of all the noble gases, only radon (Rn) poses a health hazard to humans. Exposure to radon can cause cancer. Radon is present in the dirt and rocks beneath some homes and slowly can work its way into basements and well water. For this reason, many homes have radon detectors.

If a home is found to have a high level of radon, then steps should be taken to reduce the radon. For example, any cracks in a basement wall or floor should be sealed.

Checking for the presence of radon in well water is being used as a way of predicting earthquakes. Three weeks before a massive earthquake erupted in the Philippines, scientists observed a large increase in the level of radon deep in the ground. Scientists continue to perform experiments to see if radon levels deep in the ground always increase before a major earthquake.

Why Are They So Different?

Hydrogen gas is very different from the noble gases. Remember that the *Hindenburg* was filled with hydrogen and exploded into flames. In contrast, the noble gases are not explosive. For this reason, helium can be used safely to fill blimps.

Hydrogen is part of almost every compound that is important for life.

Hydrogen is also different from the noble gases in another way. Hydrogen easily combines with other elements to form compounds, such as water. Hydrogen combines with so many different elements that thousands of different compounds containing hydrogen are known.

At one time, scientists thought the noble gases never combined with any other element. Then, in 1962, a scientist discovered that xenon formed a compound by combining with another element. Since then, argon, krypton, and radon also have been found to form compounds. Scientists have yet to discover any compounds that contain helium or neon. Compared with the thousands of compounds that contain hydrogen, there are only a handful of compounds that contain a noble gas.

Why is hydrogen so different from the noble gases? The answer to this question can be found by looking at atoms. An **atom** is the smallest unit of an element. Atoms are so small that they can be seen only with the help of the most powerful microscopes.

To understand why hydrogen is so different from the noble gases, imagine that atoms are like small, round, wooden balls. The balls act as models to show how atoms behave.

Each ball represents an atom.

Imagine that some of the
balls have a tiny hole in them.
These balls represent hydrogen

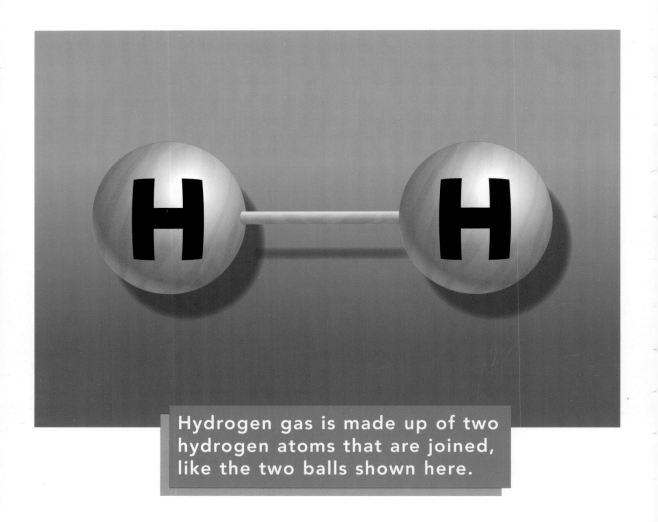

Hydrogen gas is made up of two hydrogen atoms that are joined, like the two balls shown here.

atoms. It's possible to use a thin stick to join two of these balls. It's also possible to join one of these balls with any other ball that has one or more holes in it. This is similar to what happens with hydrogen atoms. Two hydrogen atoms can combine with one another.

A hydrogen atom can also combine with other kinds of atoms to make a compound. For example, two hydrogen atoms combine very easily with one oxygen atom to become water. When this happens, a small amount of energy is released. The *Hindenburg* contained billions of hydrogen

A spark may have caused the *Hindenburg* to explode. A spark is all that is needed to cause hydrogen and oxygen atoms to combine and combust.

atoms. When all these hydrogen atoms combined with the oxygen atoms in air, a tremendous amount of energy was released. This is what caused the explosion and fire.

Now, imagine that some of the wooden balls are perfectly smooth and have no holes. These balls represent atoms of the noble gases. It's impossible

A noble gas is made up of individual atoms, like the balls shown here.

to use a thin stick to join a ball that has no holes with any other ball. This models what happens with atoms of the noble gases.

Unlike hydrogen, the noble gases do not join easily with other elements, such as oxygen. Therefore, blimps filled with helium will not explode like the *Hindenburg* did.

Fun Facts About Hydrogen and the Noble Gases

- More than 300,000 pounds (136,000 kilograms) of hydrogen are used for each space shuttle launch.

- Before launch, the temperature of the hydrogen fuel on a space shuttle is –423 degrees Fahrenheit (–253 degrees Celsius).

- Two million hydrogen atoms would fill up a space about the size of the period at the end of this sentence.

- The Black Sea gets its name because of a compound called hydrogen sulfide, which makes it possible to see only a short distance beneath the sea's surface.

- The sun produces its energy by changing hydrogen into helium. Every second, the sun produces the same amount of energy as is contained in one million hydrogen bombs.

- A blimp in Singapore contains enough helium to fill more than ninety thousand party balloons. When it is filled with helium, the blimp can be lifted with just one finger.

- A xenon projector lamp used to show a very large-screen movie is so bright that it can be seen from the moon.

To Find Out More

If you would like to learn more about hydrogen and the noble gases, check out these additional resources.

 **Books**

Blashfield, Jean F. **Hydrogen.** Austin, TX: Raintree/Steck-Vaughn, 1998.

Farndon, John. **Hydrogen.** NY: Benchmark Books, 2000.

Thomas, Jens. **The Noble Gases.** NY: Benchmark Books, 2002.

Organizations and Online Sites

Airship
http://spot.colorado.edu/ ~dziadeck/airship.html

Click on the airship on this home page to connect with a page that has many links to sites dealing with lighter-than-air craft. One link has information about building models of these airships.

NASA/Genesis
www.genesismission.org/ product/genesis_kids/ aboutgenesis/ aboutgenesis.html

The only way to know exactly what the sun is made of is to bring back some pieces of it to Earth, where they can be studied. This site contains information about NASA's plans to send a spacecraft to the sun to collect hydrogen and helium atoms that it shoots into space.

Museum of Neon Art
501 W. Olympic Boulevard
Los Angeles, CA 90015
www.neonmona.org/ main.html

Click on "Current Exhibition" to see what artists have created with neon signs.

How Lasers Work
www.howstuffworks.com/ laser.htm

Noble gases are used to make lasers, which are devices that use a special type of light to read the bar codes on products and the information stored on CDs. This site has some basic information about how lasers work.

Important Words

atom building block of an element

compound substance formed when two or more different elements are combined

element building block of matter

hydrogen fuel cell device that produces power from hydrogen

matter stuff or material that makes up everything in the universe

noble gases group of elements that do not usually combine with other elements

Index

Meet the Author

Salvatore Tocci is a science writer who lives in East Hampton, New York, with his wife Patti. He was a high school biology and chemistry teacher for almost thirty years. His books include a high school chemistry textbook and an elementary school book series that encourages students to perform experiments to learn about science. He enjoyed demonstrating to his chemistry students how helium affects a person's voice.

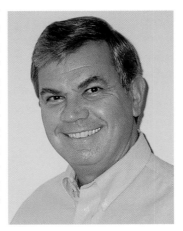